D1508975

DK READERS

Level 2

Dinosaur Dinners
Fire Fighter!
Bugs! Bugs! Bugs!
Slinky, Scaly Snakes!
Animal Hospital
The Little Ballerina
Munching, Crunching, Sniffing,
   and Snooping
The Secret Life of Trees
Winking, Blinking, Wiggling,
   and Waggling
Astronaut: Living in Space
Twisters!
Holiday! Celebration Days
   around the World
The Story of Pocahontas
Horse Show
Survivors: The Night the Titanic Sank
Eruption! The Story of Volcanoes
The Story of Columbus
Journey of a Humpback Whale
Amazing Buildings
Feathers, Flippers, and Feet
Outback Adventure: Australian Vacation
Sniffles, Sneezes, Hiccups, and Coughs
Ice Skating Stars
Let's Go Riding

I Want to Be a Gymnast
Starry Sky
Earth Smart: How to Take Care
   of the Environment
Water Everywhere
Telling Time
A Trip to the Theater
Journey of a Pioneer
Inauguration Day
Star Wars: Journey Through Space
Star Wars: A Queen's Diary
Star Wars: R2-D2 and Friends
Star Wars: Jedi in Training
Star Wars Clone Wars: Anakin in Action!
Star Wars Clone Wars: Stand Aside – Bounty
   Hunters!
WWE: John Cena
Spider-Man: Worst Enemies
Power Rangers: Great Adventures
Pokémon: Meet the Pokémon
Pokémon: Meet Ash!
Meet the X-Men
Indiana Jones: Traps and Snares
¡Insectos! *en español*
¡Bomberos! *en español*
La Historia de Pocahontas *en español*

Level 3

Shark Attack!
Beastly Tales
Titanic
Invaders from Outer Space
Movie Magic
Time Traveler
Bermuda Triangle
Tiger Tales
Plants Bite Back!
Zeppelin: The Age of the Airship
Spies
Terror on the Amazon
Disasters at Sea
The Story of Anne Frank
Abraham Lincoln: Lawyer, Leader, Legend
George Washington: Soldier, Hero, President
Extreme Sports
Spiders' Secrets
The Big Dinosaur Dig
Space Heroes: Amazing Astronauts
The Story of Chocolate
School Days Around the World
Polar Bear Alert!
Welcome to China
My First Ballet Show

Ape Adventures
Greek Myths
Amazing Animal Journeys
Spacebusters: The Race to the Moon
WWE: Triple H
WWE: Undertaker
Star Wars: Star Pilot
Star Wars: I Want to Be a Jedi
Star Wars: The Story of Darth Vader
Star Wars: Yoda in Action
Star Wars: Forces of Darkness
Marvel Heroes: Amazing Powers
The X-Men School
Pokémon: Explore with Ash and Dawn
Pokémon: Become a Pokémon Trainer
The Invincible Iron Man: Friends and
   Enemies
Wolverine: Awesome Powers
Abraham Lincoln: Abogado, Líder, Leyenda
   en español
Al Espacio: La Carrera a la Luna
   en español
Fantastic Four: The World's Greatest
   Superteam
Fantastic Four: Adversaries

A Note to Parents

DK READERS is a compelling program for beginning readers, designed in conjunction with leading literacy experts, including Dr. Linda Gambrell, Distinguished Professor of Education at Clemson University. Dr. Gambrell has served as President of the National Reading Conference, the College Reading Association, and the International Reading Association.

Beautiful illustrations and superb full-color photographs combine with engaging, easy-to-read stories to offer a fresh approach to each subject in the series. Each DK READER is guaranteed to capture a child's interest while developing his or her reading skills, general knowledge, and love of reading.

The five levels of DK READERS are aimed at different reading abilities, enabling you to choose the books that are exactly right for your child:

Pre-level 1: Learning to read
Level 1: Beginning to read
Level 2: Beginning to read alone
Level 3: Reading alone
Level 4: Proficient readers

The "normal" age at which a child begins to read can be anywhere from three to eight years old. Adult participation through the lower levels is very helpful for providing encouragement, discussing storylines, and sounding out unfamiliar words.

No matter which level you select, you can be sure that you are helping your child learn to read, then read to learn!

DK

LONDON, NEW YORK, MUNICH,
MELBOURNE, AND DELHI

Project Editor Deborah Lock
Art Editor C. David Gillingwater
Senior Art Editor Clare Shedden
U.S. Editor Regina Kahney
Production editor Siu Chan
Picture Researcher Marie Osborn
Jacket Designer Natalie Godwin
Indexer Lynn Bresler

Reading Consultant
Linda Gambrell, Ph.D.

First American Edition, 2000
This edition, 2010
10. 11. 12. 13 14 10 9 8 7 6 5 4 3 2 1
Published in the United States by DK Publishing
375 Hudson Street, New York, New York 10014

Copyright © 2001 Dorling Kindersley Limited

Published in Great Britain by Dorling Kindersley Limited

DK books are available at special discounts when purchased
in bulk for sales promotions, premiums,
fund-raising, or educational use.
For details, contact: DK Publishing Special Markets
375 Hudson Street, New York, New York 10014
SpecialSales@dk.com

A catalog record for this book is available
from the Library of Congress
ISBN: 978-0-7566-5875-5 (Paperback)
ISBN: 978-0-7566-5876-2 (Hardcover)

Color reproduction by Colourscan, Singapore
Printed and bound in China by L Rex Printing Co., Ltd.

The publisher would like to thank the following for
their kind permission to reproduce their images:
Key: t=top, a=above, b=below, l=left, r=right, c=center

Bridgeman Art Library, London / New York: Giraudon 32cr.
Corbis UK Ltd: Front jacket, 2tr, 2br, 20br, 30tc, 31.
Ecoscene: 22cb; Peter Hillme 24. **Mary Evans Picture Library:** 32tl.
Robert Harding Picture Library: 3, 15, 16tr, 16-17; Vulcan 15.
N.H.P.A.: Brian Hawks 27. **Oxford Scientific Films:** Anne Head 14.
Pa Photos: 4. **Planet Earth Pictures:** 13, 19c, 23tc; Dorian Wiesel 29.
Science Photo Library: 5; David Halpern 25; NASA 32br;
Peter Ryan 26. **Frank Spooner Pictures:** 9. **Tony Stone Images:**
Back jacket, 7. **Topham Picturepoint:** 12tc, 18bc, 32cl.
Jacket images: *Front:* National Geographic Stock: Carsten Peter

Discover more at
www.dk.com

DK READERS

BEGINNING
TO READ ALONE
2

Eruption!

THE STORY OF VOLCANOES

Written by Anita Ganeri

DK Publishing

What looks like a mountain
but spits out fire?
What shoots clouds of smoke
from a hole in its top?
What sometimes explodes
with a BANG?

A volcano
and it's starting to erupt!

The story of a volcano
starts underground.
If you jump up and down
on the ground,
it feels solid and hard.

But inside the earth,
it is so hot that the rocks melt.
The rocks are runny
like melted butter.

Melted rock

Inside a volcano,
the melted rock rises
because it is hotter
and lighter than the
rocks around it.

Melted
rock

Sometimes the melted rock
bursts up through a hole
or a crack in the ground.
This is how a volcano begins.

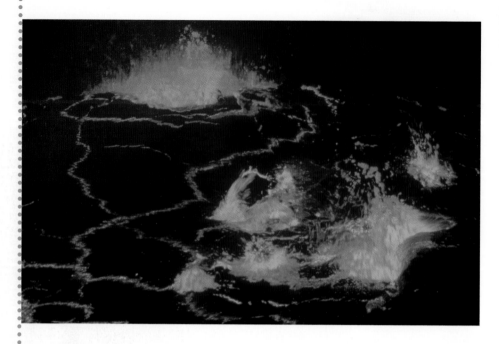

The rock that comes out of
a volcano is called lava.
At first, it is runny
and red-hot.
It cools down
in the air
and turns into
hard, black rock.

Cooled lava

Some volcanoes spurt out
fiery fountains of lava.
Other volcanoes pour out lava
in great rivers of fire.
Once the lava starts flowing,
nothing can stop it.
It can bury whole villages
and set trees
and houses on fire.

Volcanoes have different shapes
and sizes.

Some volcanoes erupt with a bang.

Hot rocks and ash
shoot high into the air.

These volcanoes form
cone-shaped mountains
with steep sides.

Other volcanoes erupt quietly.
The lava oozes gently out of the top
and spreads out all around.
These volcanoes are low and wide.

The biggest volcano
Mauna Loa (MAW-nuh
LOW-uh) in Hawaii is
the biggest volcano in
the world. It is 18,000 feet
(5,846 meters) high.

Some volcanoes erupt violently.
They blast out
clouds of hot ash and dust.
The ash is made of
tiny pieces of lava.
The ash and dust
shoot high into the air.
Some of it lands near the volcano.
It covers buildings and fields
in thick, dark gray powder.

Some ash and dust is carried away
by the wind.
It can block out the sun
and turn day into night.

At the top of a volcano
is a hollow called a crater.
In it is a hole called the vent.
Lava, ash, and dust
come out of the vent.
Some craters are many miles
(kilometers) wide.

When a volcano stops erupting,
the crater is left.
Some old craters fill up with water
to form huge lakes.
Sometimes the crater becomes
a dry, grassy plain.

Extinct volcanoes
We call a volcano that has stopped erupting "extinct." It will probably never erupt again.

When a volcano shoots out lava and ash, we say that it is erupting. We call a volcano that is erupting "active."

Kilauea (KILL-uh-WAY-uh)
in Hawaii is the most active
volcano on earth.
It has erupted non-stop
since 1983!

We call a volcano that is not erupting "dormant."
That means it is sleeping,
but it could erupt at any time.
Montserrat is a tiny island
in the Caribbean Sea.
It used to be a beautiful place
to live.
Then, in 1995, a volcano called
Chance's Peak started to erupt.

It had been dormant for 400 years.
Many people had to leave
their homes as ash fell everywhere.
Some left the island
and went to live
in another country.
It was too dangerous
for them to stay.

Volcanic ash

Mount Vesuvius (Veh-SOO-vee-uss) is a volcano in Italy.
In AD 79, Mount Vesuvius erupted violently, blasting hot ash and gas into the air.
The ash buried the town of Pompeii (Pom-PAY) and thousands of people died.
Today, people have cleared the ash away.
You can walk around the streets of Pompeii and see the Roman ruins.

A cast of a dog covered by the ash.

The ruins of the Roman town of Pompeii

Pumice stone

Pumice (PUM-iss) stone is
a type of lava. It is used for
rubbing away hard skin. It is
the only type of rock that floats.

Volcanoes can be useful.

On the slopes of volcanoes,

the soil is good for growing crops.

In some places, blocks of solid lava
are used to build roads,
bridges, and houses.
Precious gold
and diamonds
are found in some
volcanic rock.

Near a volcano,
the underground rocks get very hot.
The hot rocks heat up water,
which turns to steam.
Sometimes a giant jet
of boiling water and steam
bursts up through the ground
and into the air.
The jet is called a geyser.

Hot water
In some countries, people use hot underground water to heat their homes and make electricity.

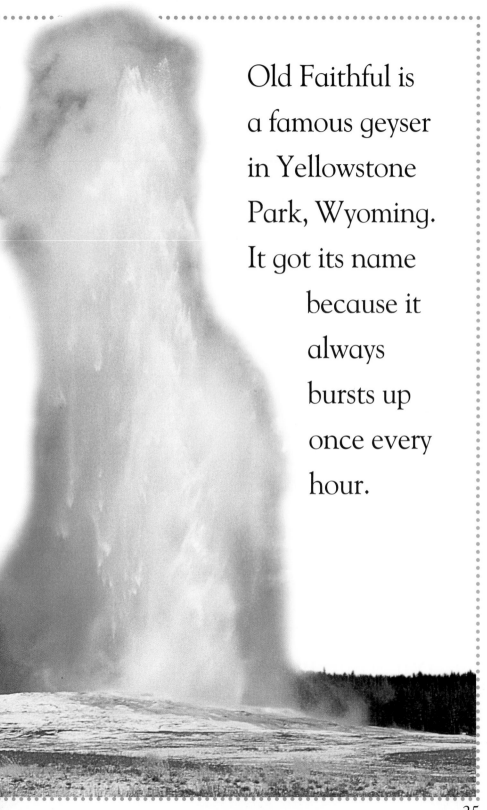

Old Faithful is
a famous geyser
in Yellowstone
Park, Wyoming.
It got its name
because it
always
bursts up
once every
hour.

There are lots of volcanoes
under the sea.
You can't see most of them.
But some underwater volcanoes
are so tall that they poke up
from the sea to make islands.

In 1963, a volcano erupted
under the sea near Iceland.
The sea started to smoke and steam.
By the next day,
the volcano had grown
and a brand-new island had formed.
The local people called it Surtsey,
named after an
Icelandic fire god.

Hawaii is a group of more than
100 islands in the Pacific Ocean.
The islands are the tops
of huge underwater volcanoes.
Some of these volcanoes have
two or more craters,
but they erupt very gently.

In some places,
lava flows into the sea
and makes it hiss and steam.
Some of the beaches have
black sand, which is made from
crushed-up lava.

Volcanologists (VUL-can-AHL-uh-gists) are scientists who try to find out how volcanoes work.

They want to know when volcanoes are going to erupt.

Then people living nearby can be moved to safety.

But volcanologists have not found
all the answers yet.
No one knows when a volcano
will erupt—until it actually does!

Volcano facts

There are about 1,500 active volcanoes on earth. About 50 of them erupt every year, but most of these eruptions happen underwater.

In 1883, the volcano on the island of Krakatoa (CRACK-uh-TOE-uh) in Indonesia erupted with the loudest bang ever heard.

The word "volcano" comes from Vulcan, the Roman god of fire.

Mount St. Helens is a volcano in Washington in the United States. It erupted in 1980 after being dormant for 123 years. The blast blew 8,000 million tons of rock off the top.

The biggest volcano in the universe is Olympus Mons on Mars. It stands an amazing 17 miles (27 kilometers) high. It last erupted 200 million years ago and is now extinct.

Index